Sibling of the Book, I'll have you know that Chariot Wish is a permutation of Revelations 19:15. They are the Page of Swords as an anarchist swordswallower, the hirsute scabbard of Eros's molten sabre, always freshly pounded to form. A phlegmatic, viscous cudgel coats their syllables, dilates the voice, & secretes a rhythmic battery of elemental images. They will tread upon the winepress of the stanza & spurt the delicacies of the verb with bubbling space. Some think 'romanticism' is some bratwurst on milquetoast stavetool overlooking a foggy mountain range. Boring. Abandon that word. Seek the Messenger. Here's a map. Trace the prairies, the bars, the boxcars, the nethers of lovers & beyonds that trail in abstract vortices which vanish like smoke. Remember: if y'all meet in Hell, it's not Hell. *P.E.A.C.E.* be with you.

—Aristilde Kirby

These poems move like perfectly terse, always revealing bulletins. Each one is loosely strung to reveal elements of a delicate and heroic portraiture. The magic and dubious romance of dailiness entwines us and begins to work as mortar. *P.E.A.C.E.* contains exquisite camera blocking in verse which calls to mind shades of James Schuyler's work. Chariot allows the lush color of life to sit and accumulate until it suddenly wants out.

—Cedar Sigo

We have before us a true poet: an artist, a comrade, a seer. Is a true poet always a mystic? Are the conversations of a poem conversations with god, channeled back down to earth for the reader to translate? "I am the speaker of the poem," admits Wish. But these poems have less to do with "confession" and more to do with what we can't know, the self that we can't see but continue to give. *P.E.A.C.E.* is an offering. In it is an alchemy: life turned to art, art turned back into a way to keep living.

–Rachel Rabbit White

Published by Changes
www.changes.press

FIRST EDITION

Design by Studio Vance Wellenstein
Manufactured by BALTO print in Vilnius, Lithuania

Changes Paperback #007
ISBN: 979-8-9889042-9-8
Library of Congress Control Number: 2024937552

The authorized representative in the EU
for product safety and compliance is
eucomply OÜ, Pärnu mnt 139b-14, 11317 Tallinn,
Estonia, hello@eucompliancepartner.com,
+33757690241. Our official distribution partner
for Europe is Antenne Books Ltd.

Changes
c/o Transport Specialties
9 Joanna Court
East Brunswick, NJ 08816

Chariot Wish

P.E.A.C.E.

A Changes Paperback

For the coming world.

Some things I do for money, some things I do for free.

—The Knife

ONE

TWO

P.E.A.C.E.

I shall not know peace until he makes love to me,
but only when he enters me and then lets me stretch out
on my side across his thighs.

—Jean Genet, *Querelle*

POSSESSICA

I get completely naked on the beach

Of course
nakedness is totalizing

Looking past the painted air
your lighthearted grief

Laughing walking into the ocean
taking my hand

This is how the world ends
This is how the world ends
This is how the world ends

NOT PEACE, BUT A SWORD

Threaded
in the morning
couldn't move
from the bed
sucking dick
half-heartedly
for two hours
everyone existed
within a world
I wasn't a part of
couldn't stop
calling to be like
can't talk to you
read about Jesus'
tight asshole
made me wet
and jealous
I wasn't the first

person to finger
the brown rose
never felt
religious ecstasy
while fucking
weep terribly
cry even harder
golden revolver
do the thing
really want
to suck dick
maybe find
myself under
the weight of
the son of God
write a map
to a cunt
you didn't
know was there
focused on
your white T-shirt

edge of the collar

revealing a chest

broke eating

duck breast in an

opulent restaurant

in La Monte Young's

dream house

talked about

public sucking

private ownership

tongue fucking

is an expression

of life's excitement

ride me all

the way out

MOLLIE'S NIPPLES

I wanted it to be done
Everything–

I wanted desire–
a sensation I was
unwilling to be moved by

I licked all I could
gold hem of sorrow
blue marble on the sidewalk
I licked it
so now it is real

There needs
to be more of me
or less

Call me and tell me
is the front door open?
I unroll a dark carpet
I walk into September

SO ARE YOU GOING TO FUCKING KILL ME OR WHAT

In God's winking eye
I kept thinking things like

This is the most beautiful I have ever felt
I want the Worm Moon to be a real worm

Have my hand disappear into your halo
you know, the one that crowned my face

before I stuck my tongue inside
Go to the beach and get ass naked

then lose my mind
Shoot two guns in my mouth at the same time

Rip the package open with my teeth
swallow the planet in one evil gulp

That's no moon
and I journey through a body

WHAT I WANT IS ALL-OUT WAR

Reaching over his waist for the fly of his jeans
Tangerine unpeeled four moons cut and halved
There is no planet Earth just a fat wet ball hanging between two holes
Take the nightingale, roll the hot part of him in my hand
We were talking about the tradition of Communists in Italy
He said, *Yea but the fascists still won*. I said, *God isn't here anymore*
Later he lifted my cunt to his tongue
Had me spit in his mouth while I jerked off over him
This is all I know how to do anymore; I take it seriously
There is no Earth, a swollen sinking spirit

I had everything
I wanted
Mouth moving
from nipple
to nipple to
nipple to
nipple
Your flesh was crucified on the body of the planet
Deep in the cellar something drips, hour by hour
held in the purple light, atoms from your
memory on all fours with a cock in your mouth
There's no such thing as an innocent landscape
What happened underneath the tree stays
between you and I
I'd feel safe
knowing
you hold
all of the weapons
Slip your hand in
pull the sword
from the lake

The tips
of your eyelashes
flittering sunlight
The piece of paper
wind torn
nailed to a tree
It was too cold
A two person job
pulling the body
out of the water

It's much better to say
I have been left here
on the side of the road
alone, ugly, suffering
than to say
What a terrible
looking hill

I DIED LAUGHING

It can enter
through the eyes
vibrations
from a thin gold chain
looped around a neck
If I was the light
I would have kept crying
like *Leave me here, in this field, weeping*
I was the light emerging
I could feel it through my panties
into the eye of my pussy
crying from the sensation
of being emptied
Two years into World War II
Mount Vesuvius erupted
Six months earlier
a popular uprising in Naples
Neighbors raided the artillery
freed their people
who were to be sent to death camps
Derek said, *how wonderful those times*
Derek told his story of dying
Derek told the story of unbuttoning a man's pants
Men are always describing
the heat of other men
Dance music played over the blue screen

like being in a room full of paintings of crashing waves
and being moved by the idea
of waves crashing
The inner experience
The inside of the experience
I'm sorry but this is how I am
Is the microphone on
I don't really know where I am
but I think I'm being punished
It's not inconsequential
this terrain
Hamlet sees the ghost of his father
I see something else
I want to be lowered into a well
understand history
Chariot, you have to be in the world today
not supine in a field
fucking
in the club
your fingers
over mine
The blood goes in
the blood goes out
that's what gives it the color
This is what the hand
that traveled through
your tunnel said to me
You are a very sad person
You had been crying
You've seen too much
though also not enough

Sick of your country
your country made you sick
There's no more money
The club burned down
Death can't come soon enough
You're giving Ark of the Covenant
The tarot deck told me
you were traveling across the sea
to a great city of finance
You try hard to survive
I'd have to put my hand
back in you to know
if you did   survive
When it's there
I'd have her say to you
Moisturize your spirit
Tilt the mirror up
Jerk the handle
Ben said *Christmas is really sad*
considering the outcome
of the life of Baby Jesus
I cry all December
at the light-up angels blowing
their light-up trumpets

When everything else has lost meaning
God, dimly perceived as love in human form
is all the meaning, eternal meaning
that we need

I couldn’t see anything
from the inside of your hair
The fountain broke
then you let it down

It takes so long, my Lord

CAN ANYONE STANDING AT THE GATE SEE?

You spit me out, I spit you out
Say to me in a curse, *Love*
I would rather see nothing at all
I would rather see the Moon
in full shine
bent and lightly walking off
the black Earth

TEOREMA

Transcendentally stoned song off a balcony
Hand through his hair as it falls on the floor
Panting on my back I said
Holes aren't longing to be filled
Oh wait, yea what about the one
stretched so far over night
slouched in your dimming light
Crying while making out
with the most beautiful man
Terminal walk up a mountain
Grace of degeneracy
being the body around an anus
Wanted to pee on you
in a loving way
worse loss of all
Wet arrow to the back of the head
Why this urgency
Unrolling the length of your jouissance

Don’t know what the deposit body of the Earth is

Fags know death

Live close to death

The shape of your neck is real

This kind of waiting

is the love itself

I don’t care what you meant

A long black glove slides over history

The eye takes the picture
The eye keeps the memory
Your long ankles crossed at the table
Your hand pulling at the skin on your neck
A divinity is circling over us now
Light one candle for money
Another for jewelry
House   Weapon   Fire
The holy holiday of Friday
Sounds out the darkness
Steamed Earth split and milking
gray quarters of the sky

In this dying world
all fantasy withers
under the weight
of reality
Actually
the eternal soul isn't
wretched and it is
the greatest joy
to be in the space
of totality—

An angel slices through

I take myself on the bed
panties at my ankles
stir my pussy with the air

A decaying body

An infinite spirit

O Sunshine

in an empty place

Now the cherry tree
covers the bluebells
A memory of history
seen from the inside
of a wizard's sleeve

Pussy out on the train
I haven't been the same

The difficulty faggots have in existing is a blessing.

—Guillaume Dustan, *Nicolas Pages*

Her first night in New York
SoHo was on fire
God splits our skin
with a big nail
plunges in a dirty hand
There are no angels
in America
passing through the exit
wound of history
Why didn't you tell me you like violence
I like violence too
In this place love
is the most wicked thing

The Information Wars
Celebrity socialists
Businesses that sell weed that doesn't get you high
Dating apps
Internet porn
Chatbots
Starbucks union busting
Uber Eats
Race fakers
Beyond Meat
Asexual flags
Viral videos of peoples' meltdowns on airplanes

January 6th
CHAZ
Gangstalking conspiracies
Pro-ana communities
Doomsday cults
Hype Houses
House hacking

The Mennonites smelled so good
so earthly their bodies
naked under
blue and black clothes

Give it one long lick along its heel
The big container
The fattening sky
I've made ancient Greece very small
Now I will eat it

Over the ocean
I thought about
peeling the night back
exposing the raw air
to wrap us all up in it
the deep cloth of night
We could wear it like a shirt
crouching in a doorway
for some crooked version of salvation

In the dark of something burning
I thought about putting
my hand through the night
tugging it down
and wearing it like a shirt

GODSTAR

A great wind was at my back as I climbed up the stairs
I imagine now that we share the same mouth
When I'm sucking cock it's your tongue
guiding me up the nodes of skin
Everything I taste now you taste too
as if there are multiple worlds transposed
a net over the singularity of my vision
My throat a doorway for you to enter through
Our friends could let me wrap my lips around their ear
like a conch shell, what they would hear would be
the the slow pulsing of your breath a heartbeat knocking back
When I saw your face and nothing was left but your face
We flowered into a wound marked upon the world of the living

There's this disgusting need for my forehead to glow
to transmit that energy my thousand-year-long stare
to the tiny detail of your eyelid, a gate of creased skin
When you extend your spirit through night to me
it's the cool shiver of my fantasy about
the filmmaker and the novelist touching each other
over me, through me It's almost a river, this motion
pulsing my fingers in bed
Beautiful machine, a torch, a cross
Every star is throbbing
pouring from the dish
Almost, then barely exploding

SEVENTH VEIL

How many times did that hole overflowing blink at me
Open bare all teeth tongue
on the shore there was a guy
with binoculars pressed to his face
while he tugged his little pecker
to the other man getting photographed
in underwear

Your name was Aubrey, I didn't have mine
Just sat in the audience
drank coconut water from a box

We submerge ourselves
where we are
confused & decorated
His silence
is a three-letter word
caught in the ear
of American metaphysics
This coil wrapped
so tight
There is a light
in my window
I follow it
all the way
You found me

licking salt
from the butterfly
What glows beneath
embroidered
in our magma
is human desire
and life itself

The misty dream in October
black diamonds on a rhinestone bag
You promised to go on

*

A vapor
across the street
A glimmer
in the bathroom mirror

CUPPING YOUR HANDS

Cupping your hands in the fountain
your wings on the air
The sun tipping into Virgo
on Coney Island the ocean
was a hot dark mass
You shimmering
in the dense jewel of it
Blood Angel
of the bath in the Earth
The wings of your voice cornsilk
licking the air

We talk about what the planets are doing to our hair
What the corn harvest is like this year
Jupiter's words, a disco in the tall grass
You're cupping your hands in the fountains of Earth
Your hands on my oiled pearl

In the morning my hair is like
the Spiral Jetty
secret and perfect
and dovetailed

ARE YOU HAPPY HERE, IN THE WORLD

Psychic mirror

Sacred playhouse

Magic stick

Sleeping on the air

isn't exactly how it sounds

it would be

In the morning

when I flood back into myself

I'm rocking on the corner

of the universal body

The sun is

a soul

in an egg

on fire

I feel outside of the world

taking the train

through the hole in the day

It's crazy how normal this all is

Fucking in the night

I think it's beautiful

I feel ugly under the moonlight

Around 5:55 a.m. the sky looked

neon green and disgusting

We're all ugly in God's eye

HOPE THIS SEASON OF LIFE FINDS YOU WELL

I take all that I can fit
from the soft hand of the sun
How can I behave with the Earth like this
birds spilling out the hothouse of morning
At the beginning of Earth
there was a hole in the ground
in night's
darkness
there was a hole
splayed
out and open
It was night's
tiny darkness
coming through
It's a hidden place
where people go
to hide bodies

my eyes won't stop funneling
information into my brain
The dimensions are falling apart
a portal is blooming
there was a hole
pee-spangled
shining
pulsing
heavenly hot
secret root
wet heart
the open nerve of Earth

*

I took out a little boat
prayed between the days
Why did god make me perfect
beautiful and insane
like a blizzard
This is what I need in life

it was the birth of the universe

and I was by the ocean

fussing with my hair

*

You were always on my mind

*

Bondage Dominance Friendship Money

I feel the influences of the planets

I'm being whipped sideways

Naked in the prairie

I'm whipped by the left leaning light

I wanted to come out from the other side

a fountain at the beginning of Earth

*

Play this song at my funeral if I have one:

In the fabric of night there's an entrance where the grass lifts

up in fountainous weeping light and there are 7 doves in the sky floating like pink ribbon. I wonder how many years it will take for it to disintegrate

silk slapping the air at all hours. Time is a ritual. A ribbon in the wind

*

You might be by the ocean

Me, I'm licking the juice from my wrist

Me, I'm on a boat

I'm underneath the trees as well

Come into me deeper

Look for me here

the inside of your car

Where will you spend eternity

*

You be good

See you tomorrow

I love you

Moon is huge tonight petrichor the wet god rail
I have this feeling it is moving its tongue
or hair wrapped around my silly neck
the train worms its way through the bridge
stupid fog machine won't stop blasting........fog
You can't talk like that because you weren't there
when the oceans were created Ok, yes I was
How about you give me my turn to rip my head off its shoulders
throw it like a pumpkin from the highest tower of the castle
If heaven is belief in the future then tell me
which line to cross to no longer be a virgin
Like where is it hidden in the circle of your breath
I'm falling ill with some incurable beat
while a maiden sticks her finger into the gash
underneath my nipple in the shape of a star

SEX CHANGE

I wanted to suck the egg
I couldn't find the front
I thought I was going to
fall into the black toilet
My new body sees things
the old one could not
It's a secret that I'd share
but it is mine
Gabriel
is a deserted island
uninhabited by our
Abstractions Affirmations
Automations Attributes
Appetites Affects
Affections Aspirations
Analogies Actions
Beauty Beings
Doings Boredoms

Cities Capacities

Causes Definitions

Deaths Durations

Determinations Desires

Encounters Errors

Essence Fictions

Finalities Freedoms

Images Intellect

Ideas Ideals

Longings Infinites

Knowledge Laws

Methods Needs

Literature Bodies

Mind Modes

Necessaries Natures

Negations Numbers

Order Passions

Powers Signs

Rights Reason

Societies Songs

Kinds Virtues

Wounds Thinking

Substance Compulsions

Feelings Agency

Repression Sexual

Health Families

Masturbations

Obligations

COMMUNITY ACTION CENTER

What god or angel would look to see this
Me living with everyone who is dead around me
Could gut myself like a melon watching
one dyke sew feathers into the ass of another
This is on loop in my mind all week
Facing the city backward
there is never anything
but the distance sometimes
This is the web of everything
One fist inside a body
inside another
sprouting to a wing
I feel this beat all week
I cradle joy like a dove
preening feathers
counting each unit
The inside and the outside
The back of my neck

has a spirit that says
It is not enough to fuck
To feel the pulse
of everyone dead
in the yolk of desire
The East River's
a discordant sex
Time has broken over
the bone in the world
It's not enough
just to want
The erotic light
flies into energy

I felt the spirit of the air
on the back of my neck again
Is this time or a recording of time
bare ass through a cloud
pearlstringing in the dead at night

The wind interlaced
with suncrowning Earth
Suncrowned hill
I'm not sure if it is time
that comes to fill the distance
between a planet and a star
Open air crowning
the wind on my neck

In the dead night there's the Moon over looking hell on Earth

YOU PASS THROUGH ME

Blood that collects the surface
Blood that jewels the thick skin of reality

A good girl can only be one thing
a Good Girl

Sometimes to sleep
you have to become ancient

to maintain a mysticism
I protected the thick skin of reality

I felt so much pleasure
molecules around me convulsed

My personal quality of horror
A blood of braided revenge

an infinite chain of losses
I felt so much pleasure

when you cried
When I made you cry

when I let you make me cry

Which way is north
and to what tower

The one that sees
The one that sees

A VULGAR WIND BLEW

A silver wind blew
as you left the room
In the reflection of the pool
I was watching you
lie down in the water
I was watching you
feel the river
It was a long black hallway
wait no—it was red
Time poured through
all of the lines
which led to this
Each time it is the night
hot tears shiver from my face
On a burning pine
what shudders in
divine imminent death

Rain moaned over the scene
Black net of pigeons stretched
Diamond-crusted morning
Empire looks so
grotesque
I can feel
my organs
stacked
like wet stones

The poverty
of your absence
makes me rich
War revealed
crimes revealed
reality enters
where the eye
meets the mind
Dark Halo Energy
destroys the city
Some live to endure
human mechanics
Others are spread
across
a destroyed city
Jehovah
guides
possessions
possessions
imitate
love—
a dark halo
energy spreads
around the eye
Impaired seeker
Impoverished soul

sucking
each ring off
each finger
one by one
ten by ten

This century will not heal with the fields

The land will heal when it wants

Your agony reminds me of mine, can we talk

Sibling of the Book, I hope you're doing well

There are times when I look above

and beyond but I do not see

COOL MY EYES

In the between months I was not there
the burnt $5 bill stayed on the bookshelf
There was a postcard that was a picture of nothing
laminated black marked “LA at night”
You were away, I was sleeping on the couch
I wanted constantly to know where you came from
You were so beautiful driving home soaking wet
Okay, I was trying to be drawn in like going toward
what I want rather than letting it come to me
The dark chest of your cunt
I wanted to be fucking in a way that left
no trace of the self in the action
The bathtub mists in the dark
I can’t stop being in my life
But that’s not what the poem is about

DOUBLE PENETRATION

God

spent

years

becoming

The Book

I have

to slide

through

the keyhole

It will

become

night

Of course

we

are

all

talking

about

the sky
opening
up
Where
else
would
it
come
from?
There are
souls
leaving
the
Earth
Seed
hidden
in
the heart
of
an apple
I keep

my treasures

in

my ass

Only

a simple

charming

replicator

could have

the electricity

of

the nation's

demons

Strapped

to night

delicious

movement

joins me

When

was Jesus

crucified?

A long

time ago

in

the

place

called

the

skull

Let us love this distance, which is thoroughly woven with friendship,
since those who do not love each other are not separated.

—Simone Weil

P.E.A.C.E.

I was lost in the beauty of the Marxists
I was afflicted in their affliction

In the pit of our century
there was peace, sometimes
under the shade of a tree

I was writing a poem
How beautiful that sun
how beautiful the planet
that circled

It was going to destroy me
and still be beautiful

I had to disappear into the word
so she could retrieve what was left

The daylight
The voice
The fountain breaking
The space
between
the navel
and the heart

Long-winged
in the corridor
of planetary
alignment
We come to Earth
in the vulnerable body
of a peasant

The Law of the Book
is the law of reflection
The one that
becomes two

God is turned
Turned my face
from the heavens

Earth from
the heavens
in this way

The bread kept the pearl

The pearl kept the secret

The lost riot

The lost world

Can I bear them

Carry them all the days of old

Of course we are all talking

about the sky opening up

Where else would it come from

The flood

The futile

The fetid

The flood

The flood drank the river

and moved on

Spent some time

in lonely places

Asking God for, tell me

is this how the future

will remember us

The mountain air

sanctuary

behind the curtain

Piece of a song

heard through the window

It was my heart that dovetailed
over our heads all I could see
was that love has three eyes

One that sees, one that knows
One kept shut for the stone inside

If I reached the peak of a mountain
I would simply turn around

If we meet each other in hell
It's not hell

What has found me
What of me
remains unseen

Everything
looks like I'm seeing
through a silver eye

It will become night

I’ll have to slide

through the keyhole

Breakable gate on the ledge

Fat sky delicate trap of mountain

Machine wrought grass

Crown of the earth sucking water

Irreverent bird

Chaotic sky

Silly poet

Knocking back gorgeous & foolish

Pooling from the rift between

the creature and the creator

David sat us down
to give us his prayer

He said, You remind me
of my brother
who died of AIDS

There are coins falling
from the hole in the sky

A volcano weeps down
the edge of its own face
beneath Earth's dress

I felt like a piece of torn silk

An aging dove

At the intersection

of two competing

spiritual events

History is a medical record

A voice

through a cloud

The eternal skirts by

Love slopes

from the pissing moon

God spent years

becoming the Book

My own element

drowns this bright spot

this side of a world

You drive your car
around diagonal winter sun

It was never hard
for me to look at you
It is really hard
to not be looking at you

Wild shade of night
Shade of eternal night

Dirty sun weaver
beautiful anarchist
against the glass
fingers deep
in the hot blooded Earth
little silver earring
the color of night

Hold it like a mirror
that you can taste
wield it like a whip
follow it with tongue

Heaven bent

Turned night

turned day

turns night

The ocean

in the depth

Her skirt

torn through

the heart of land

Water filling

the crotch of day

is jammed into

wind of Friday afternoon

Radiant head of God

rising hot

Fire swallows
all of this sickness
burning out of the hill
where sky meets grass

A thousand summers over
unraveled
on a dawn salted corner
wretched from the night

It's been an awful century

The ring falls out of your eye

I see only in light

I want Jesus to forgive me too

Totality isn't weeping anymore

and the Moon

is rising the hill

There is a soul
on the naked shoreline
A single star
in a line of trees
I couldn't say what it was
that I had wanted
Singing the song
I didn't know the name of

The world isn't a wound
even when it looks like one

Heaven, Martin Wong

NOTES

The poem "I Died Laughing" borrows the lines "Leave me here, in this field, weeping" from Federico Garcia Lorca's poem "Ay!" and "It takes so long, my Lord" from Nina Simone's song "My Sweet Lord/ Today Is Killer"

The poem "Teorema" is titled after the Pasolini film

The poem "Earth Will Break Your Heart" borrows its last lines from Corona's song "Rhythm of the Night"

"In The Nest of Spiders" references the title of Samuel R. Delany's *Through the Valley of the Nest of Spiders*

The poem "The Unblinking Eye" borrows lines from Tony Kushner's play *Angels in America*

The poem "Seventh Veil" borrows the line "Human desire and life itself" from Felix Guattari's essay "So What"

The poem "Intelligent Dance Music" borrows the line "Heaven is belief in the future" from Robert Glück's novel *Margery Kempe*

"Be Thou My Vision" is titled after the Julius Eastman composition

"Community Action Center" is titled after the film by A.K. Burns and A.L. Steiner

"Get It How You Live It" borrows its last lines from Janet Jackson's song "Together Again"

The Poem "Hope This Season of Life Finds You Well" borrows its last lines from the last words of Alex the grey parrot

The poem "Double Penetration" borrows the line "I keep my treasures in my ass" from *Towards a Gay Communism* by Mario Mieli

ACKNOWLEDGMENTS

Some of these poems have appeared in various forms in *The Quarterless Review*, *Shitwonder*, *Columbia Journal*, *April April*, *Tiding House*, *ITERANT*, *SARKA*, *Blush Lit*, and the chapbook *A New Heaven and a New Earth* (Wonder, 2021).

My deepest thanks to Bennet Bergman for seeing my vision and bringing this work into the world. Eternal gratitude and fellowship to Isabel Boutiette, my editor and sister in poetry. Thank you to all of my lovers and friends who have had me while writing this book. To all of the elders in this world and to those who have gone to the next, thank you for the light forward. Thank you to Cool Memories, Poetry Field School and the Naropa Summer Writing Program. Thank you to all of my students over the years. Thank you to my beloved co-teacher Ben Fama. Thank you Nata Perla-Ward, Arthur K, Matthias Kodat, Rico St. Rico, Amara Daxx, Adam Green, Sif Artoria, Marcus Scott Williams, Theo Thimo, Omi Ashauer, Shy Watson, Marty Williams, Ivanna Baranova, Maya Martinez, Jordan Sullivan, Dylan Spencer, Mannat Kaur, Garrett Phelps, Anabelle Declement, Elissa F, Jenny Ryder, Oyster Kim, Joshua Atwood, Magdalena Gallen, Trinity Noone, Naomi Heron, Kelpy Cathedral, Ted Dodson, Dave Morse, Manel Kara, Jesse Prado, Zoe Breszny, Daisuke Shen, Tara G, Mohammed Zenia, Eduardo Pulgar, Smith McLean, Aristilde Kirby, Tommy Cook, Willow Wilderness Hour, Cedar Sigo, Rachel Rabbit White and Nico Walker: Without your conversation, love, and example my life and work would not be possible. Forever in memory of Mego Saienni.

$24.99

ISBN 979-8-9889042-9-8